I'M TRYING
TO TELL
YOU I'M
SORRY

I'M TRYING TO TELL YOU I'M SORRY

NINA
BOUTSIKARIS

xoxo

Black
Lawrence
Press

Black
Lawrence
Press

www.blacklawrence.com

Executive Editor: Diane Goettel
Book Design: Amy Freels
Cover Design: Zoe Norvell
Cover Art: "Photosensible" by Alexandra Levasseur. Handbuilt ceramic, glazes, underglazes and oxydes.

Copyright © Nina Boutsikaris 2019
ISBN:978-1-62557-713-9

Published 2019 by Black Lawrence Press.
Printed in the United States.

While this is a work of nonfiction, names and some identifying details have been changed or concealed to protect the privacy of some individuals.

"To learn to see the frame that blinds us to its interiors is no small matter."
—*Virginia Konchan*

Contents

Be My Nepenthe

Let me explain the situation. Last fall I flew to Miami on someone else's miles, some guy's black American Express card. He asked me several times and finally I decided to see what would happen. I mean I knew what would happen. I knew what I would probably have to do. What I mean is that he had been a friend in childhood, a boy who once showed me how to slide down his parents' carpeted stairs in a sleeping bag, and though we'd lost touch for many years I let him fuck me on his roommate's green satin daybed in the West Village one summer when we were still in college, which was charming because we had so much to reminisce about and because he had lots of money—a useful illusionary tool for a brief encounter. Other people's money was not something I had really thought about before, not to such a degree. But then I was on a plane from New York to Miami with a company-paid ticket folded in my wallet. I bought new underwear and sharpened my eyeliner and stuffed it all into an overnight bag. My ass cheeks were burned pink from a tanning bed. I did these things and I watched myself do them. I considered my performance, just as I always had.

What this all really means though is that I was worried. His friends were models; I'd been eating a lot of chocolate and bread soaked in olive oil with cheese. People kept having these end of summer parties with good cheeses. I had been sick for a year, and now I was feeling better. (You look healthy, one nurse had said, sucking blood from the crook of my arm through a tube and into a vial.)

The kid picked me up from the airport in a silver BMW and the weekend passed as slowly as though we were children again.

Meaning very slow indeed.

I tried to make jokes but he did not think I was funny. He took me to expensive places in South Beach through a side door, which is all he had to offer, and I listened to people who looked like him complain about each other to each other. Someone told me I was lucky to be there. I smiled and accepted a bump of cocaine and drank enough tequila to think that maybe I wanted to fuck one of these people.

3

What I'm saying is that I tried hard to make it okay, but I couldn't. Not for me, the object, let's say. Not for him, the subject—slippery as that might be. But let's just say.

This was new. What I mean is that feeling. The unease.

In the cabana-themed bathroom I called a friend who lived in Coconut Grove, but she was out of town.

Meaning that night I had to do what I had to do. To be gracious, to at least try. It was among the less easy encounters. I really had to will myself not to think thinky thoughts about objects and subjective invest-ments, about spectacle and the big, black void between us, the melan-choly in the reification—thoughts that made me sad because I knew I could probably never unthink them; that there was no going back.

Back at his condo I sat on the kitchen counter in the half dark-ness and drank more wine while he told me how everyone loved what he'd done with the place. He asked me if I liked his vintage leather sofa: Isn't it good?

Norwegian wood? I said.

On the sofa I made some sounds from my throat so he wouldn't feel too bad. Or so I wouldn't feel too bad about the decisions I'd made, or the failure I was to us both.

In the morning I got dressed and sat outside on the small bal-cony and asked for coffee. He had none.

I don't drink that, he said. I've just never needed caffeine. Do you want an acai bowl? A green juice?

I was starving. I wanted a pretzel croissant. Wanted to be alone. But not why you might think.

What I mean is I was disappointed in myself. I was surprised.

I'd never failed at pretending before. In general I'd say I had a handle on this kind of emergency intimacy, how to create it in a hurry and hold on in bursts. I'd say that, at one time, it was my best thing.

I used to have such a good imagination. I used to be so tough.

I opened his fridge. It was all beer and hot sauce and tiny con-tainers of salad bar accoutrement.

He had very, very little to say.

Meaning the discomfort was now full blown. It was an unavoidable crisis.

I watched him pick up a tiny roach from his bedside table, spark it with a white lighter, and close his eyes.

At the airport I walked up and down the halls with my overnight bag. I ate a Klonopin and bought a hummus wrap and almost cried because I knew I hadn't taken from him whatever he needed taking. Not the way we both had hoped I would. Not the way we had planned. I had broken the contract, failed to be the promise, the desire, the notion.

Maybe—here's what I mean—I'll start over.

Maybe this was now my newest best thing.

—

Like Derrida says: *The archive has always been a pledge, and like every pledge, a token of the future. Archivable meaning is also and in advance codetermined by the structure that archives. It begins with the printer.*

—

Nepenthe:

1. /niˈpɛnθiː/ (Ancient Greek: νηπενθές) a medicine or potion to soothe sorrow, a "drug of forgetfulness," or the plant yielding it, mentioned by ancient Greek writers as having the power to banish grief or trouble from the mind, depicted as originating in Egypt. Literally, the "anti-sadness."

2. Anything inducing a pleasurable sensation of forgetfulness, especially of sorrow or trouble.

If I ever have a daughter will she hate me if I name her that? *Nepenthe*, the anti-sadness. Could she ever forgive me for asking her to take it all away?

The text beside the painting praises the artist's use of subtle symmetry and lyric line. The text says that subtle symmetry is a perfection so beautiful it makes one forget all pain. The way the artist has soaked the paper red so that the pink edges bleed, then stain, then fade to yellow; the way there is that smudge of lichen green.

I suppose it could.

When you get down to it, everything is just some shade of vagina: folds of blistering red or midnight navy or that cotton pink bleeding into yellow. Look next time. That's all the world is made up of.

Once I fell in love with a man because he used the word vagina regularly, sometimes more than once a day. It was really something.

Once I fell in love with a woman who avoided it.

In the museum, two couples. Old friends. The men wear khaki shorts and shirts tucked into belts. The women in their clean, white athletic shoes and cropped hair dyed an impossible color. One of the women looks up at the blue Rothko and backs up slowly, carefully, until she is in the middle of the room, until the concentric blocks bend beyond her eyesight. Until some of the blue can no longer be metabolized. She moves deliberately, as though someone once told her to do this. Pace by pace.

The other woman stands beside a man who is sitting on a bench, folding and unfolding his baseball cap.

She says, They really do have some incredible work here.

I can't hear the man but already I can see the woman looking like she is trying not to need him. Looking like, I will be ok.

Women, with all their expectations! Just like our mothers. Fathers might be a little disappointed deep down, but mothers! They won't stop doing that thing with their voice until you know how bad you've hurt them. They're all, Why don't you love the museum? The mausoleum of the looker, the gawker, the gaze.

But the man is done. It's Friday for god's sake. The game starts in two hours and we're tenth in the nation. He wants to walk the clipped lawns of his alma mater and remember. Who could blame him. The woman is trying so hard with her jaw and her eyes. Look at the art. Look at me looking at the art. Look at it with me, why don't you. Everybody went to Paris to copy everybody else. Even us. But you sat a lot then, too. You were so easily tired. I wore stripes. I got a little fat.

–

Renoir's preferred subjects were adolescent girls, whom he ideal-
ized as perfectly epitomizing female beauty. He wrote: *In literature as
in painting, talent is shown only through treatment of the female figurine.*
    Here. *The Sculptor in His Studio.* Behind his head a woman wiggles
in front of a window above a city, her hands covering up or playing
at the place between her legs. Maybe both. The sculptor looks out
from the canvas with black hole eyes, holding a tiny replica of the
woman in his hands. His tiny, tiny woman. He made this tiny tiny,
this subtle symmetry.
    She wasn't much, but she gave him that.

—

Our mothers tell us, Be my nepenthe. Lovers ask us, Are you my nepenthe? Strangers, the most, need us too. Meaning on the street and in the coffee shop or at the bookstore or in the park, they expect it. You should smile more. You'll get ugly if you don't smile more. Smile, sweetheart. Smile for me. Make me forget. I'm saying the forgetting is something big. Something more than a bad day, a lonely evening. I'm saying the forgetting is about sickness and death, the abject; mortality. The stuffing away of something spilling out at the seams. A tidying up.

Yesterday in front of the co-op a man rolled a cigarette and scolded me: Didn't you hear me? I said I like your bike.

I could see how angry he was.

Later, I admit, I was a little sorry that I could not help him. But I was tired—he smelled like soggy cereal.

Another day, another man who looks at me and sees, perhaps, a bit of nature, a pastoral scene.

You must be on your way to yoga, he says.

What? (This is an accident. It just comes out.)

Aren't you on your way to yoga?

Um, I tell him, juggling a bag of damp vegetables, a yoga mat, water bottle.

Well excuse me Miss Rude, he says.

I mean, he is offended. And really it is my fault because today I do not have the energy to explain it. To say that even if his intentions are merely inquisitive, if he just really needs to know for his own peace of mind whether I am going to yoga or not, my skills of flash differentiation are sometimes too weak to separate one uninitiated observation from another. To explain how difficult and time consuming it can be to tell when an exchange will turn. And yes there is a part of me that wants to ask him for forgiveness, for not having the patience to see when this specific turn will come.

Just now a man passing in the street tells me I am doing okay but that I could use a little more ass.

A man outside of a bar tells me to keep it up.

Keep it up, baby, he says, and then he claps. He claps!

I move through a life that I am only pretending to lead, filling time in an attempt to cover up my true identity as that which chases away sorrow. Go to work and to the store and other little places like that in disguise. They all know what I'm up to, the power I can wield, the potion I am keeping from them.

Give me your potion!

(This is the background noise. It's very loud.)

—

Some days, though, no one needs me to smile or to relinquish their grief, and it's those days I feel the weight of it the most. What am I to do then?

—

Was I ever not afraid of men? Of other peoples' fathers: good-look-
ing, clean-shaven, socked-feet up on an ottoman, fishing olives out
of martinis and yelling at the television. Of dentists, not the drills
but the eyes. Of doctors and their gloved fingers.

Meaning did I ever not fear that they would and would not?
Even before my hips got wider than my waist and suddenly boys
twice my age were asking did I know how to suck a dick without getting hairs caught in my braces. Boys, men, always asking me to keep
secrets. Meaning I spent a lot of time sneaking around. A lot of time
playing Juliet, playing Maria, in someone else's personal tragedy.

But that's what I liked most. The rush, I mean. I liked hiding.
Liked lying. Liked organizing my secret worlds.

Meaning I still do.

What I really mean is I wanted them.

And I thought about it even then, how betrayal isn't always
betrayal. That no one else deserves every part of you. Even then,
when I was fifteen, when I'd make my boyfriend tie me up and lick
ice cubes off my stomach on his mom's silk sheets, I would sometimes
let this other boy, this older boy, buy me a poppy seed bagel at the deli
and pin me down in the back of his Jeep until sixth period was over.

Or later how I'd tell another boy—the one whose parents hated
me because I was still in high school and he was twenty-two, still living at home, stinking up their certain kind of organized garage—to
drop me off at the top of my street, nights when we'd been out doing
stuff in empty corporate complex parking lots and in the wet grass.
I'd wait for him to drive away and I'd walk to my neighbor's house
in the dark (this really beautiful guy) and scratch at his bedroom
window. We'd smoke a little joint and my eyes would close and I'd
let him do his thing.

This is how I did everything. A few in my pocket. My secret
entourage.

And I've never told the whole truth. Not to anyone who's seen
me take my clothes off.

I told most of it to one boy, a boy I once thought I'd end up being a certain kind of grownup with. What I mean is he was not outside of me. He was not separate, not like everyone else. The one I forgave when he did the kinds of things I had done (because who was I not to forgive). Most of it. But not all of it. Not since I first started getting coaxed. Not since the time someone told me, meaning someone who shouldn't have been telling me things like this, that I was lucky to have a pussy that tasted like butterscotch.

Not since the first time I felt somebody let go of his weight when he put his mouth on my mouth. When I was basically still a kid. When I was still pretty happy just being a kid.

Not since I saw what I could make somebody's eyes do.

Those sounds.

I'm trying to tell you what I was taught.

There was before and there was after.

Meaning I wanted to know what everyone's spit tasted like.

I mean prying open mouth after mouth.

I'm just going to say it. I wanted to know what I could make other people's mouths do.

So this is what it all meant. How in middle school I'd sleep over at this girl's house whose older brother bought me red underwear. And how when that girl was asleep I'd crawl into the room where the brother was waiting in his boxers, chewing gum.

After those kinds of nights I wondered how people went about their days like everything was normal. I wondered how people could think about anything else at all. He pushed his fingers inside me until I bled, like he was prepping my body for some other body. And that was good enough for him. In my ear he whispered things like, no one will ever keep us apart.

Which meant don't let anyone find out.

I lied so much then. I pretty much became a liar right then. But you know what I'm going to say: my parents found messages on my computer all about what he wanted me to do to him. Things that had to do with my hair and much more graphic things.

I tried to run away. But it was winter.

Meaning I was only gone for a few hours before it was cold enough to go home, back to my mother with the printed pages in her hand.

Which meant he wasn't allowed to talk to me anymore. He blamed me for my carelessness. Which meant he was ashamed.

A few weeks later he was back with a girl who was his age with long legs, ash-gold skin, and cleavage pressed in place like fresh-made jam. And when I tried to confront him in the school parking lot he twirled his keychain lanyard around and around—something older kids with cars always did with keychain lanyards, something I could not wait to do someday—and the circles got smaller and smaller until the lanyard was wrapped tight around his fingers, and the keys hit his knuckles and bounced and stopped when they lost their centripetal force.

Still, he filled a page in my eighth-grade yearbook with hearts and Shakespeare.

This was good stuff. Meaning new ways to control. Meaning being controlled.

What I'm trying to tell you is that there were many of them and there was only one of me. One was going off to college when I was starting ninth grade. He was someone's stepson. We slept in the same room for a few nights in the family rental on Cape Cod with the rest of the kids—because we were all kids really, except for him.

Meaning we snuck around. Like how in the dunes he untied my Old Navy bikini top and traced the tan lines it had made. It was us against everyone else, us hiding and professing. When we left at the end of that week I was hysterical. Which looked like me falling out of my dad's car crying when I read the note he'd written me: *Don't worry, I will never forget you even if I get a girlfriend at college. i love u QT. C U soon.*

And at summer camp, the counselor whose fingers were between my legs in the dim red light and chemical air of the darkroom. His hands up my shorts while I scrubbed silk screens free of ink, rubbed my own hands raw with orange exfoliate soap meant for tools. In my bunk I'd write letters to some boyfriend at home telling him I was lonely without him. Which was true.

What I'm saying is I was distracted. I was always distracted by somebody's hands, or when there weren't hands and why not. Names in cryptic ink all over my Converse high-tops.

—

My mother was beautiful when I was a child. My mother was also sad. This is not a huge surprise, not such a rare thing. She needed something from me that I did not know how to give. Not the way she hoped I would.

What I mean is once I was like a potion, a perfection so beautiful it could make her forget all pain.

But I fell away, inside my teenage self. And she tallied up my absences, holding tight to the lack.

She asked me things like, Don't you want people to like you?

She said things like, Pretty doesn't last.

You need to work on the inside.

You need to work on being less self-involved.

I often stood outside myself and tried to see what my face was doing, what my body must be doing, how my voice sounded, until I thought I probably understood what my mother was saying. I probably seemed as though I was someone who needed nothing. Which is in fact an overcompensation for needing far, far more. It is easier to need nothing.

My father was a little mean, but not as mean as me. My mother reminded me that unlike her I was vain, and had been since childhood.

Which wasn't untrue.

The first time they took me skiing I spent half the morning throwing a tantrum in the parking lot because of the bulky snowsuit he stuffed me into. I was six and thought people would think I was fat, that they would see a girl made out of puffy down and not the very small person I really was underneath. My father didn't understand how I could possibly think something like that.

How can you be so difficult? he shouted.

At least once I stayed home from kindergarten because none of my socks matched. I cried and screamed at my mother until she shut my bedroom door and told me to go back to sleep. For hours I lay on the floor watching the morning explode outside my window.

I cried again that year when Miss Carla revealed a painted model of the human heart, a red and blue upside-down pear the size of her tan fist, bulging with glistening veins—compared it to the sparkly rubber charm hanging off my backpack and everything was wrong. How could it be so complicated?

—

When we desire an object, we expect that it will remain an object. But a lot can happen to mess that up. The object might look back, might also want something, might know what it's doing and how to get what it wants. Or maybe it doesn't know, it just wants. It wants what you have. Or it sees what you want. Or, mirror-like, that object reflects the fragility of your own subject-ness. Look at you, with your desperate desire turned inside out.

—

I got a little older, meaning just a very little. I was still really young. Young enough to mess around with boys who thought they were grownups messing around with young girls. Like this one at my high school whose job was to push TV carts around.

Meaning he was a college dropout. He was in a band and had robot tattoos and wore a lot of cologne. He had a dimple in his chin and we, meaning teenage girls, wanted him.

Which meant I learned where and when the security guards were on duty so I could sneak past them through the unlocked door of the light booth above the auditorium, dizzy while I waited for him in the dark. In my ear he would whisper things like, what am I going to do with you.

This went on for months. On and off for a year. Maybe more.

What that all comes down to is this: one day he told me I bored him. People were watching us. It was my fault. He told me I was ruining his chances with other girls. So I tried to starve myself. Stood in front of the mirror looking for what was wrong—what mirrors are for, the usual things.

For a while I avoided certain hallways, took the long way around to get to the science wing. Until one day I forgot—perhaps I was thinking of the future—and there he was, leaning on the doorframe asking me where I'd been.

Which meant I was powerful again. Which meant that I wasn't.

Meaning after my English test I would follow him up the hill to his room with the Tibetan bedspread where I lay on my back in the June afternoon because I wanted to be enough.

But he was not real. Meaning he was real.

I mean it was humid, it was almost summer, and he was sweating through his red tee-shirt from the walk, and we had to be quiet because he lived with an old Polish woman who was watching daytime television in the white living room with her small dog on her lap. I looked around at his things: notes he'd left for himself on yellow Post Its, a framed sepia photo of a pretty girl on top of a mountain, his bong and his dirty socks hanging off a mesh hamper like worms. And even though it was very hot I shivered.

Once in spring, when I was fourteen, two boys in matching oxford polos drove up to my house in a shiny silver car. It looked brand new and they smelled the same artificial way, or maybe the way a Ken doll would smell if he were alive, placing his plastic hand on your plastic thigh. My dad was in the front yard weeding around the lilac bush. The lawn was muddy because my father didn't care too much about grass. The boys asked him, did I live here. He left the front door open and pretended to do something in the kitchen. I didn't know who they were. Maybe kind of, but not really.

Remember, they said, at the dance?

Something about meeting their friend.

I didn't remember, they weren't from my school. I didn't know how they knew where I lived. On the porch steps we talked. They tried to get me to go to a party.

Who were those boys, my father asked me. He moved some pieces of mail around on the dining room table. I didn't want him to worry so I made something up that sounded simple, even though the whole thing felt much more complicated, like a thing that he probably would worry about.

The boys came back once. Again they asked me why I wouldn't go with them. Really it had something to do with feeling like that if I left the porch at some point I would let them down. At some point they wouldn't want me anymore. I wanted them to come back but I didn't want to have to go, and when they never returned I knew I had done something wrong. Hadn't been the kind of thing they needed. I never understood how they knew where my house was.

–

Renoir's son claims that the painter once told a journalist, *I paint with my prick*. Though the *Oxford Dictionary of Quotations* argues that what he really meant was, *It's with my brush that I make love*.

—

The irony of the painting is in the title: *Man Greeting Woman*. Kiff, 1965. An orange blob, leaning forward with purpose, tipping his hat, beckoning with his hand. The Woman, paler, is naked too, but she's on the ground, startled and loose, as though she has been awakened from a dream. Surprised, bemused. She looks inviting. She does. She's not saying no. Once her function might have been to sync the threat of her form with carnal excess. Okay, in preliterate western societies gender images were performative—they spread the news, circulated social roles, enacted religious meaning. But what's changed? Adam hides only his eyes while Eve covers her breasts, the curls of her pubic hair, with both hands. The places where leakages might occur, the threats.

Maybe it has never been me looking at myself. Where or how could I even begin? A man is greeting a woman. And so she is naked in a field.

–

In elementary school I sometimes got in trouble for taking off my shirt. For gathering an audience of little boys, all elbows and collar bones and smooth skinny legs, outside the swimming pool's cinder-block changing room. How someone named Miss Sharon or Miss Kelly, who wore Birkenstocks and a brown corduroy vest, would move quickly to help me back into my Green Eggs and Ham tee shirt and usher me inside. How I knew this meant I was doing something right, something girls were not supposed to do, and then must do.

One Halloween my mother helped me dress up like Amelia Bedelia, the maid from a series of children's books, who took every-thing literally and got everything wrong. I had just learned to read and she made me laugh. My mother sewed a bonnet and fastened plastic flowers in place with a hot glue gun, finishing in time for my school's parade. In my blue and yellow classroom she helped me change into a long sleeved leotard and a long skirt. Three other girls were dressed as Jasmine. It was Jasmine's year. I watched them lin-ing up by the door in their gold tiaras and plastic sandals and blue crop tops. They looked so right. And their mothers were there too, sweeping handheld camcorders back and forth.

As we lined up to make our way to the big tree house, where prizes and candy would be handed out for our transformations, I slid the sleeves of my leotard down over my shoulders, exposing two pale rounds to the Pacific autumn air. But my mother saw me and tugged the cloth back in place.

That's not how the costume is supposed to look, she said.

And maybe that was fear—those first glimpses of something fall-ing away, coming loose like feathers: one here, a lonely artifact on the first grade classroom floor.

It rained all through my twelfth October, letting up on Hal-loween. I borrowed some black lipstick and a sequined mini skirt from a friend and slipped into a pair of cheap gauzy wings. A high school boy with a bad crew cut and a mysterious scar on the back of his head pulled me along ahead of the others. The streets smelled of pumpkin guts, wet leaves clogging the gutters, and oily tar. I tucked my frizzy hair behind my ear because I knew I was being watched. That summer my mother had caught me touching my hair when our waiter dropped off a plate of crispy calamari and glanced at my exposed thigh.

She's aware now, she said to her friend, tipping her wine glass in my direction. But she had forgotten how long ago now really was.

—

Cheng writes, *The act of painting seizes power not by dispelling threats, but by giving form to terror and desire.* We don't take control by seeing, she says, rather, we are the ones altered when we look.

—

Here is Oenone in the forest on Mount Ida just after the sun has set. Oil on canvas. The painter is Henry Augustus Loop. The year is 1879. The plaque beside the painting calls it somber and refined. The plaque states that the painting *demonstrates the 19th century tastes, which included mythological and classical motifs.* The Greek myth goes like this: The nymph Oenone was so angry with her mortal husband Paris for betraying her with Helen that when Paris was fatally injured in battle she refused to give him her lifesaving potion. She sent him back to Troy, potion-less, in a rage. But when he died, Oenone was filled with enough regret to throw herself into the funeral pyre where Paris's corpse burned. Or hang herself. Or throw herself off a cliff. Depending on which version you read.

Before her suicide she considers what she's done—withholding like she did. Considers forgiving him. That's when we find her here. Heavy-lidded eyes, red lips, the tops of her classical ivory breasts, exposed and glowing, glowing and soft beneath the shadows of the trees. The body sexed-up with subtle reveals, with illumination. At first it appears as if light actually radiates from inside her. Perhaps, though, she is lit from the reflection off a pool of water at her feet, or from one faint shaft of dappled light in the upper right corner.

Consider the symmetry of her nose, her jutting hip, waist emphasized by a rope belt, the way the fabric is draped to reveal. John Berger notes that in defense of the expression of European humanism, Enlightenment artists believed that ideal beauty could and should be constructed. Why not take arms from one woman and the torso from another? Let's celebrate the viewer's desire. Let's celebrate the looking.

It's hard not to wonder what parts from what women went into the making of Loop's Oenone, a nymph who kills herself to atone, to apologize, for not saving the life of a man who started a war over the beauty of another woman.

This is supposed to be a tragic scene, a moment of regret. But isn't she beautiful? The artist can't help himself. He can't, he won't, separate her body from the story. As coy as she is, as innocently rendered. And wouldn't Oenone be happy knowing that? Wouldn't she be grateful to the painter? Even Paris could love her now, after what the painter's done to her.

—

Maybe what it comes down to is the difference between the goddess and the permeable body, *a body that confesses its lack of stability*, writes Posner. Like Kiki Smith and her leaking humans, refusing to behave, stoically revealing their private humiliations. Squatting, dripping milk and blood and urine. Posner wrote of Smith's sculptures: *These women reject the graceful refined poses of western statuary and startle by performing private acts in a remarkably public and matter of fact manner. These are sexual beings, not erotic objects.*

—

There is risk in the self-naming, the looking back, the acting out: parody and spectacle just appear so much alike. In other words, if she is a certain kind of girl, won't she always be a certain kind of girl? It takes work not to get turned on by the violence of expectations. Anyone might trip up, might look at subversion, revolt, and still see an object. (Who are we kidding—she's fuckable or she's not.)

—

I heard him over the music—everyone did, because he wasn't trying to hide it when he leaned over, shoved his hand up under the hood of the pizza box and jabbed another boy's shoulder, a boy I called my friend.

Look at that, he said to my friend, Just picture your cock sliding up into that fat pussy: just, like, this.

And he squinted, moved his hand like a saw, back and forth, as you and I walked across the room.

He was very serious, though he smiled at something beyond both of our bodies, beyond the stinking, crowded room, the frayed navy carpet.

I stopped going where I was going. I looked at the boy who was my friend. He was looking at his own jeans, picking something off the hem. I looked back at the other boy. And then I heard my own voice, felt the veins in my neck buckle with blood. And I guess I didn't handle myself very well, not the way you should handle yourself, so of course he called me a fucking cunt, stood up from the sofa with his dripping food and his eyes like milk and screamed you bitch shut the fuck up you fucking prude cunt over and over while his face went wide and blank with fury and there was no one else speaking or moving, just the boy with the milky eyes and me.

It seemed to go on for some minutes, this diorama, this still life of what people did and how things were allowed to be, until you reached for me, until you pulled me outside with a red cup of beer still snug in your hand. I followed you down the hill to somewhere else, another party, I don't remember. You knew where to go. You told me to hold your cup while you tied your sneaker. But I couldn't stop shaking.

You looked so beautiful in the sudden darkness, your hair still wet from the pool. Like a swan. And I wondered was it courage that made you laugh? At him or at me or at all of us? Or was it something else?

But I guess that's what you are supposed to do. That's what everyone said later, when they told me I must have really needed to get something off my chest, and, Are you feeling better now?

Because it was my anger, don't you see, that had caused the trouble.

For a long time I held my keys between my knuckles when I passed that house.

In the museum I watch women. Women holding onto their elbows, a fist on each hip, looking up at the archives, the overwhelming presence and absence.

When I grow up I want to be Tracey Emin, with her spread legs and her abject desire. I too want to give it all away, hand it over, reach through. Isn't that what I'm best at? Isn't that what they've been telling me? Embarrassment and rage. Accusatory and sentimental. But which is worse?

Barthes knew: *It is no longer the sexual which is indecent, it is the sentimental.*

I confess I am not above the perversion of feelings. I confess there is pleasure in the effects of the feelings themselves.

See what you did to me? See what I can make you do? Look at it with me why don't you.

—

There were many others. I mean on the outskirts and some at the center. This is all to say that I've collected them. I seek them out, ones who likely also collect, ones whose long hair I can tug when they are still asleep—you know what I mean, the kind of earned intimacies that take time, that you can fake if you have to, if you're in need of that kind of thing—and in their ears whisper stuff like, I know I'm not supposed to think about you but I do. And they'll be the kind of boys who might say something back, like, I think about you too, while their eyes are still closed, still heavy with something they put in their mouths a few hours ago.

Meaning I'll need to leave.

What I mean is before it gets not real. Before I am real. I'll need to be quick on my way out so they don't think I want anything else, and in the dove-colored flurries I will take a taxi I can't afford back to my apartment and eat cereal and look at my clothes on their hangers and in piles on my bed and think about what to wear the next night and hope that I am still my most wanted self so that when we are both feeling powerless or powerful we can find each other again. Or not.

And that's the point. I mean these are the things I've learned to expect. And because of certain things I lost some other things, being distracted.

Meaning I was born, like those who are also born this way, with certain desired and hated commodities, maybe the most desired and hated commodities.

By which I mean being a kind of girl. And you know that's what you are because they won't let you forget, not when we're young and certainly not when you're older. They won't let you forget what you're worth and not worth. So one thing that might happen is that you might test it out. You might test what you can do and who you can do it to. You might test everyone around you until you have a menagerie set up on your windowsill or wherever you might want to look at it.

Meaning I've kept it intact. I still polish it, still oil it to ward off rust.

I'm not the only one who has ever said things like this. And I'm not the only one who at some time has wanted to be eaten alive by a stranger. Or by someone who only wants spit and sounds. And maybe we reach for it or maybe we let it happen. Because somebody, maybe a lot of bodies, will have taught us that there's this balance between good and bad. That we have to do it for them. That we aren't good if we aren't bad. But if we're bad, well that's worse.

Which is all to say it's not unlikely that at some point I will want it all, the thing I need to know I am still capable of getting, and I will take it. And it might mean that I trample on someone like him or her or you, someone who means more than sounds and spit. Or maybe I won't know the difference anymore.

Meaning it isn't totally my fault.

Which also means I'm sorry.

Which doesn't mean I want to take it all back. Not all of it.

—

Derrida calls the archive a site of amnesia because it destroys memories in the very process of selecting and excluding what will be
remembered. *A site for disorientation.* A site for control, in other words.
Flaws and mistakes make up the records.

So let me just set the record straight: I am the villain.

But you probably already knew that.

—

There's no real ending in writing about your own life. Only segments of examined companionship that by necessity come to a close. What that means is the possibility of redemption continues beyond the last page. Forgiveness, maybe. For how I will make you stop loving me. How I'll lose sight of the notion, already a ruin of what you have decided me to be.

Bourgeois wrote in her diary: *I want to be transparent. If people could see through me, they could not stop loving me, forgive me.* As if writing it all down was enough of an apology, a good excuse. As if being the recorder could make anything forgivable, make anyone lovable.

I get it. I do.

—

This One Long Winter

I've been ill for three months and I'll be ill for three more. Six doctors can't find what's wrong with me. At their smallest, each tonsil is the size of peach pit. I chase antibiotics with steroids, with big white doses of ibuprofen, with sugary homeopathic pills that dissolve into the walls of my cheeks. Nothing keeps the suckers down. I want to yell at people on the subway: Can't you see I'm choking? Random foods make me puke. Yesterday it was quinoa. Quinoa! A shiny, wet rainbow across the bathroom floor. I can feel my own abjection; a leaking rupture, a permanent shift: the daily fevers, the night sweats, the nausea, engorged and cratered tonsils anyone might catch sight of if I open my mouth too wide, the sensation of chewed food clogging up my throat, the paranoia of sudden onset fatigue. It takes hours to leave the apartment. Each day before waking fully I take my temperature and gargle with salt water and spit and feed myself two aspirin and some applesauce from a jar. Then I sit in the shower until I feel like I can stand.

Some mornings I'm too weak to leave, so instead I float in the backyard where a widening lake has been growing and growing between the buildings. I let myself bleed into the lake, brush the cloudy red plumes from me like bothersome seaweed. I drift on my back and raise my eyes, listening to the traffic over the Triboro, the soggy winter pavement. I watch for planes. I wonder about pilots, why they don't narrate the journey more often. (…*to the left is the lake where I learned how to swim; and those circles of light down there come from this; take a look at the Mississippi; take a look at the border, the desert beneath us; is anyone from Denver? Go ahead and wave to your hometown.*) Do they think we're not interested?

How much slower and louder the world goes and goes—and does it still go?

Like Woolf wrote: *Illness enhances our perceptions. We float with the sticks on the stream; helter skelter with the dead leaves on the lawn, irresponsible and disinterested and able, perhaps for the first time for years, to look round, to look up—to look, for example, at the sky.*

And maybe that's not the worst thing.

–

Give me more tests, I tell the doctors, but they say they have no more tests to give.

So I take matters into my own hands. Every few weeks, once the relief of my last negative test results has worn off, I walk ten blocks from my office to the free clinic in Chelsea, where men with dirt-caked blue jeans and sores around their mouths hang out, and I start the harrowing process all over again.

It's cold and most of the patients in the basement waiting room wear puffy navy blue parkas over their tee shirts. They look hungry in more ways than I can begin to imagine. A television hanging from the ceiling is silently tuned to the local weather channel.

There is one woman, alone, with hair down to her calves.

She watches me from across the room. I've seen her before, but can't place where. The days are like dreams, both watery and vivid. Everyone looks familiar.

Slow down, she says. Be softer.

That's nice advice, I think.

I sit on a plastic chair surrounded by baskets of free condoms, use my tongue to dab at my gigantic tonsils while I text boys whose last names I don't know. Boys listed in my phone as SohoHouseBryan and TallMarco. I want to know if they've had tests. I want to know what is wrong with them so I know what is wrong with me. Mostly no one responds. They are nighttime people after all.

The nurse who takes my blood is the same one every time. He likes my veins.

Nice big veins, he says, laughing. You could have a lot of fun with those.

Once, while I'm waiting for my third round of needles, I show up at the clinic director's office—a cinderblock room with barred windows, an ancient, hulking computer and rows of mint green file cabinets stuffed with death and good news.

I've been waiting two weeks, I say. I'm desperate.

He's sitting in a chair behind his desk talking to someone with a clipboard, but he lets me in, looks at me, soaking wet from the rain, and smiles.

They would have called you by now, he tells me. They prioritize the sick.

And sure, the test—each test—is negative, but I'm back at the end of the month still scared.

At night, if I'm feeling well enough, I force myself to run the treadmill, to burn off the angst I accrue sitting at my desk, answering emails and pitching health books to the same public radio producers over and over. Once in a while I actually doze off while I'm stretching, facedown into the ripped blue gym mats, their foamy insides bursting out in crumbled chunks.

My white blood cell count creeps higher and one doctor tells me over the phone that it will be time for an MRI if I'm not feeling better soon.

Soon? I think. I could be dead by then.

—

The abject is the thing we find repulsive, the thing that is cast out, ignored or pushed away in order to preserve our corporeal selves as safe, as healthy. Normal from not. But I'm not sure I can tell the difference anymore. Kristeva says: *The abject is the thing that disturbs identity, system and order. The thing that does not respect borders or rules.*

Throat, what are you up to? No one seems to know. What rules will we break, this perverse throat and I.

—

The worst part is that it comes in waves. I stop eating at the table with the healthy and instead—from somewhere down the hall, through the rushing blood in my ears—listen like a fish in an aquarium, while others chatter softly and whine and scrape their knives, t's and s's slipping downstream.

But some days I feel pretty good. For instance, I'm going to get a cavity filled this morning and last night I was out until three a.m. being skinny and sick and chain smoking cigarettes on a frozen rooftop bench because I have nothing to talk about to anyone anymore. I'm consumed by the mystery inside me; my body is so small one doctor weighs me and mumbles, Good Luck.

The nighttime is the hardest. Something about how quickly the dark comes down (comes up?). I'm prone to anxiety, to claustrophobia and agoraphobia. But I'm also anxious about being alone.

A boy I knew from my hometown was behind the DJ booth—someone's older brother whose mother once taught dance lessons in her home. I was wearing nothing: a pink bra, something white, some boots. He called me over before I left with my coat over my shoulders and kissed me on the mouth like we were old lovers.

Oh mama, he said, two hands on my face like he really remembered me, like I had always meant something to him.

You got better, he told me.

And I knew what he meant, too.

—

The dentist tells me I need Botox in my jaw.

Do you clench? he asks. You bite in your sleep, don't you?

He's a huge man stuffed into baby blue scrubs. Black wrist hairs push through his snug gold watchband like determined grass and brush my face as he fastens the crepe bib around me.

I nod. I guess so, I say.

On the wall is a framed photograph of a school of tropical fish. Beside it is a big tank of real tropical fish, blue and yellow, swimming in loopy circles or bobbing gently against the glass walls like little buoys.

I guess I bite in the day, I say again, sort of testing it out, tapping out a rhythm with my teeth.

I recommend Botox for that, he says. Relaxes the jaw. Take the edge off your jaw there.

He reaches out and touches my cheek, strokes my jaw line with the back of his finger.

Your jaw's got a masculine edge, you know?

He spins my chair until I'm facing a small square mirror.

Give you more of a soft, feminine look, he says, reaching out again with a scratchy thumb.

But I can't see my reflection, there's nothing in the mirror but more fish. And now I'm looking around for other women to compare my face to, or to save me from him, I'm not sure which. When I check the mirror again, there she is, the woman from the clinic, perched inside the fish tank speaking very slowly and loudly, her eyes like saucers.

Are you ever going to stop being someone else? she says. All around you is softness, waiting. But where are you? You don't think it's possible to release all your old words and now your throat is shutting down. Just listen. Maybe tattoo the word soft on your forehead, she says.

She's pissed. She leaves through the window.

Not today, I tell the dentist, so he shakes his head and quietly fills the cavity.

Later with the DJ I have dolmas and beer, pumpkin pie and wine, pot, cigarettes, gin and sushi and more gin. On a rooftop in Alphabet City I tell him about the Botox dentist and we laugh. But still. At some point we're at a bar in Brooklyn with a floor made of sand. I knock over a bowl of toothpicks at a restaurant and get rushed out. I ride on the back of his bicycle down Seventh Street, across Tompkins Square. He pulls up my skirt in the basement of Ella, pushes me against a pyramid of tied-up trash bags, against the ladder that leads to the street; I blow him under the DJ booth while he's working, in the bathroom on my knees, in the cab with his best friend in the front seat reaching back to touch my thighs. I want them both so bad: the anonymity, the oneness, all of it—the immortality of nighttime.

My tonsils ache. I swallow and swallow and swallow but my throat is too dry; it remembers everything.

You have the most perfect body I have ever seen, the DJ tells me. Where have you been? Where have you been?

He doesn't know about the woman in the fish tank or the clinic or the doctors or the lake behind my apartment. I'm the one with the secrets. I'm the one with the power. Something happens in the language and gesture of these kinds of encounters, the kinds I can control. Something magical. I am together and alone, untouchable and exposed. So all I can be is proud. And I am so, so proud.

When I get home the next morning it's snowing. I sit on the sill in front of the fire escape and gargle warm salt water and watch a man in a camouflage cowboy hat hoist a heavy black garbage bag from his yard up into a second floor window on a rope. He speaks Spanish to a woman above. She takes something from the bag when it reaches her and then he lowers the bag back down. Then he pulls on another rope and a different plastic bag rises, a white one, filled with what sounds like one hundred glass jars. He passes the entire thing through the window to her. They have a system. When he's finished, he climbs up the fire escape ladder and unclips underwear and sheets from off a clothesline before the freeze gets to them. He surveys the plot, canopied by crispy vines and the quiet, empty branches of one dark fig tree. The snow is turning to slush and soon it will be rain, because it is only early November after all. A child moves a faded pink curtain aside and watches me for a moment before she lets it fall again and moves back into the apartment.

—

I can hardly fall asleep anymore without the paralysis kicking in—napping my way through Sunday after Sunday, passing out before dinner and waking in the early hours of the morning, drenched in sweat. Just as I sink something else whirs awake, something crunches, explodes from the center of my skull like it's trying to escape; my ears ring and buzz with the vibrations of one hundred tuning forks. Then there is the waking world: the soft gurgle of the humidifier, the shifting bronze light; buses wheezing in the street below, the songs of city sparrows. Through a scrim I see and hear it all. What comes next is someone else, pacing or whispering—floorboards creak, weight compresses the foot of the bed, pushes air around the room until there is a breeze, until the tremors inside my skull begin to subside. I'm stuck somewhere I shouldn't be, somewhere I'm not wanted, in a space only I know exists—jaw locked, arms pinned against me like an invisible cocoon.

I worry it will happen in a stranger's bed. I worry about what my face must look like, contorted, teeth grinding.

Hunched over a blue screen in the dark I enact my nightly ritual, searching for groupings of symptoms, adding sleep paralysis to the queue. I learn this word: *Hypnagogia*, the state we pass through to and from sleep, which we only remember when something goes wrong, when the curtain falls and we are privy to the seam, to the secrets of our own unconscious movement.

I call my brother at college because he says sometimes it is the same for him: waking up paralyzed, body tugged between here and there. He is the only one who understands. Scientists say the intrusion of REM-related motor inhibition into waking consciousness causes a transient hybrid between waking and dreaming. But these aren't like dreams. This is much more tactile. There may be some unfamiliar conscious awareness, they say, of typically non-conscious hyper-associations between motor-related memories. Things like fear and touch. (Fear and touch: what else?) But finally there is very little scientific explanation for a phenomenon that people can't help to verbalize with supernatural imagery.

We talk about this instead of my infected throat, the fevers, the blood tests. We talk about this like it's a strength, a superpower. About folklore—the Jungian archetypes; the Intruder; the Stranger; the German "witch presser," Hexendrücken; the Polish zmora; the "old hag," who sits on sleepers in Newfoundland; the Old Norse mara; the dead baby kokma in the West Indies; beautiful Lilith, who seduces both men and women; about the third eye and electricity—and we think maybe we were on to something.

–

Sophie and I kiss in the basement of the Maritime Hotel and I want her so bad because I know she wants me back. We fall over each other like dead rabbits in fake fur coats on our way to her friend's apartment uptown where someone plays show tunes on a piano all night long.

On the street men say things like, No fucking way.

Surprise, I want to yell.

At the bars, the nighttime boys ask to take pictures—underfed and towering in black stilettos and matching leather jackets. It's late November. We are broke and always cold. We pass out in her bed on frigid Friday mornings and her alarm wakes us up two hours later. She prods me with her skinny limbs before leaving for a waitress job. I listen to her feel around for her bra, her hairbrush, her eyeliner in the dark. She takes everything into the bathroom and kisses me goodbye, still stinking of stale cocktails.

I wear her sweaters. She buys me charcuterie and cheese plates and fancy yellow wine at Eataly. It's been years since I let myself touch meat but with her I eat prosciutto, use my tongue to hold it against my gums and nibble the paper-thin fat. I sleep between her legs like an old tortoise, like we are the only ones left. A new mine to hack at, a well of becoming more or becoming something else, something not so utterly on its own—illuminated by the fragile mystery that is my unwell body, the one thing I've come to love.

It's just us in the backseats of taxis, and us with tiny drugs tucked into our boots, and us behind fitting room doors in department stores, sucking down shot bottles before it's dark out, smoking and smoking until we can't talk—I like to go places where we don't have to, where we can't. Where it's just us and everyone else.

–

Kristeva says it's neither object nor subject, but instead lurks some-where in between. *The abject body violates its own borders, disrupts the typical wish for physical self-control, for social propriety.* Instability and vulnerability ensue when boundaries are under threat.

But I don't want borders anymore. I don't know how else to express it. I've never known how to feel close without doing some-thing wrong.

In Hinduism they say the throat chakra is affected by how clearly you are able to speak your truth. When it's off balance your whole body will feel it. You might find yourself lying or doubting others. You might feel isolated and misunderstood.Physical and emotional infections can accumulate.

It is my fault. Everything.

—

What we liked to do once mornings had grown thin around the edges, the sun sheer like white linen and gone by four o'clock, was to put on eyeliner and these old fur stoles she had collected from thrift store heaps during the years she'd been living on Avenue C before me. Which she liked to tell people. Which really meant something to her, to live there.

But we were both good at collecting. I had a habit of taking the long way home so I could walk alone up Seventh Street and stop in thrift store doorways to look at the dusty furs and rows of soft plaid shirts, brush my hand along the racks of used clothing, spin the belt wheel and finger the jackets, the cracked worn leather of someone else's life.

If I'm being honest I loved the way those old animals smelled the most. Sort of thrilling in their strangeness and still so much like a memory. A phony nostalgia. The smell of once having been looked at.

On lots of nights we'd throw them on and then what would happen is we might walk together, arm in arm, down to Tribeca Grand or someplace easy like that, where one could slip inside without a wait, without any kind of trouble, where there'd be girls from Long Island and finance boys.

We'd have some gin. It didn't take much to be the people we'd quietly decided we were. To do what we did without having to talk about it.

We'd lean across the bar, say hello to the bartender if we knew him, hold our drinks close and look around at the shiny crescent moon groupings of silk blend shift dresses and patent stilettos.

And if there was a purse left on one of the tables—one pretty enough to see in the darkness and small enough to hide beneath the fox around our shoulders—she would pick it up and push through the crowd, down a hall with high ceilings to one of those dim red faux-boudoir powder rooms, where middle-aged women in uniforms hand out paper towels and mints—stuff that made me sick when I thought about it, even though I still went to these places and checked my reflection in the oval mirrors those women wiped down. Even though I still checked to see about my hair and if I was thin enough.

Without stopping, one of us would go into a stall and count the cash, if there was any, flip through keys and iPod play lists, slide open the tube of lipstick and dab it on our own lips—test its texture. No one should leave a bag out like that, not here, doesn't she know?

When it was all over, one of us would tuck it under our arm and we'd walk back through the hall, grazing our fingertips along the gilded wallpaper, until we found the coatroom or the lobby where we'd lay down the keys, the wallet with the money inside.

Someone dropped these, we'd say, because those things did not matter.

It was the trappings of someone else's expensive mouth we wanted. It was just the taking.

On the street corner we were women with other people's objects hidden beneath our coats. We were just two women making a getaway.

It wasn't until the taxi ride home that we'd start passing the thing back and forth between us. One by one we'd toss the remaining belongings onto the backseat so that in the morning the purse would be empty on the floor of my room. And when we woke, it would wink, light catching the metallic details in this lovely, hopeful morning way. We'd cover our mouths and look at each other, pushing something down, down back into our guts.

It was the eyeliner, she'd whisper. It made me mean.

The apartment was always hot, the air close. Roaches scattered from the stove and the windowsills when I turned on the bathroom light, whispering around the rim of the trashcan. The fan ticked forever with something that was caught inside. Beyond the sheet I'd hung to hide my bed and desk was a sleeping boy I hardly knew, a boy with sunken eyes who came from the Black Mountains and wanted to be a painter, but instead worked at a coffee shop in the neighborhood and got into fights.

Someone should have it, I'd say, it was your idea. We'd talk in voices not our own to make each other laugh, laughing ourselves into sweaters and sandals, out into the cold that was colder than it had been, so that our toes went gray and numb. Down to the street, humid air popping through our cheeks, sputtering in front of the man behind the counter when we tried to order coffee. And then it wasn't funny that I couldn't find the thin air with my lungs. That I was sweating from weird places: the insides of my wrists, my shins. That the shop was too warm. That the steam and the milk and the churning grounds smelled like garbage.

Then I was outside, holding onto the lamppost and crying. I mean heaving, like a lost kid. These weren't my lungs, really, these weren't my ugly gasps. It was as though they were being expelled from me. Vomited up. Like I was simply a vessel for someone else's life.

I don't know how else to explain it.

I'd put the paper cup on the curb and squat down and keep my eyes on a puddle for a long time before she'd reappear next to me.

I'd try not to think about what we had done. Who we were. I'd look for something very real: the brown smudge of a soaked napkin floating near my shoe.

People puffed morning cigarettes, hunched over crossed legs—breath and smoke together fogging up their bluish faces—and watched me in the way that people in this town are good at watching, like they want you to know that you aren't there at all.

–

If you look inside the throat, past the tonsils and into the vocal chords—the parts that move when we sing—you can see it, this muscle, gripping and opening. Koestenbaum says: *Everyone understands genitals are mythologized, but no one talks about the doctrines clustered in our throats. How do we talk about what the throat knows and suffers?*

It looks like pleasure in there—the glottis is a slick orchid, folds parting with vibration. *And like any pleasure, so much can go wrong. Know too much about the throat,* he says, *and you'll fall silent.*

—

Sometimes on my lunch break I stop by my mother's studio on 36th Street where she teaches Meisner and scene study. I like to sit in the dark and watch her students feel, their raw empathy, perspiring under the harsh black box lighting. The smell reminds me of childhood, falling asleep backstage in New York theaters; musty dressing rooms, latex, makeup and sawdust. It's a complicated comfort.

One night someone in a white tee shirt follows me into the back stairwell when I sneak out between Chekov scenes. He hands me a composition notebook and tells me to write my number in it. I've seen him in class a couple times, working through bits of Sam Shepard—crying and cursing, wiping spit from his mouth. He's tall with thin lips.

You're so cute, says the actor, peering down over the stairwell railing.

I meet him the next night at some surf themed bar where his friend works. He's carrying a gym bag over his shoulder. We compare our arm muscles. I can see the blue in mine. We take shots. I'm thinking (is this all I'm ever thinking?) let's just get to the part that's coming.

We ride the subway to his aunt's pre-war apartment where he's housesitting. He does that eager thing people sometimes do when they want to pretend they know someone. Sometimes that's nice. Sometimes it's just what it is: look at us rushing towards the fix. Lately, though, I like to wield it when I get bored, to swiftly take down a tedious, temporary facade with something real, something banal or domestic and vulnerable. For instance, I might make him meet me at the grocery store so he can watch me pick out fruits, smell the navels of cantaloupes and squeeze avocados, hold up packaged wholegrain crackers and read labels, count calories, decide what to put in my fridge. Watch me shop for what I want, what I actually need, something he could never understand. It works every time. We'll both cringe, he'll disappear, and later I can cry because I'll never be what he wanted.

The actor stares at me on the crowded train until I stand on my toes and kiss him. I push into his hands so he can feel my ribs through my sweater. I make the sounds. As if to say, everything you imagined is true. Everything they told you is real.

It's so easy.

The actor's aunt was a ballerina and the hallways of her apartment are heavy with photographs of long, thin dancers—fingers reaching, feet stretched. Their calves like polished marble. The actor pours us some whiskey or something and talks me through a few of them: this is her with Baryshnikov, this is the American Ballet Company, this is Vienna. Everyone loved her. I mean everyone. Look how beautiful she was.

I don't know about dancers, I say. My dad loves a dancer and she'll never leave her husband.

Suddenly he gets very serious. My last girlfriend was a dancer, he says. I loved her.

He wants to prove how tragic ballet can be. He's planning, assuring me we'll go to the ballet when his favorite ballerina is dancing.

I'll probably cry, he says. I always cry.

One outstretched arm is holding him up, palm pressed into the wall somewhere between clusters of frames. Meanwhile, I'm trying to work out who I am in all this. Not the dancer, certainly not the beautiful aunt. He hasn't asked me one question. He's only told me what he sees.

Kiss me like you did underground, he says.

So I let myself sink. The delicious warm goo of intimacy, real and imagined. Of something I don't even want. A second piece of pie. A sugar sleep.

In his room there are three huge potted plants. I tug gently on the leaves of one of the ferns, feel its compressed mass like candy fluff in my hand.

There's a glass case on the floor, too, with a chameleon inside named Maryanne.

Look, says the actor, turning on the heat lamp and stroking Maryanne's back. Her eyes are closed and she doesn't move. A few brown crickets bounce among the wood chips at her feet. We fuck without turning on any other lights. He keeps whispering about how he wants to take me somewhere. Costa Rica or something. We lie in the weird orange amphibian glow and he holds both my hands and asks if I'll take care of his plants for a month while he goes to Baltimore.

It's just an understudy job, he says, but I can't turn it down. He puts his wet mouth on my forehead. My eyes are closed. We'll drive them to Queens tomorrow in my car and they can be all yours for a little while. How does that sound? Would you like that? And I guess I would because that's what happens.

But before that—before I get into his Camry with the plants and ride across Manhattan; before he lugs them up two flights of stairs and lingers a little too long and tells me he can't wait to get back and be with me; before I realize that I will have to be very cruel very soon—I wake up freezing and damp with fever, a strange clammy arm slung over me. My back is burning; the stubble of his shaved chest has rubbed it raw. It's too much. I throw up in the bathroom, rinse my mouth, put on his shirt and get back in the bed.

When I wake up again it's late morning and the actor is gone. On the kitchen island he's left an apple and a packet of Dora the Explorer fruit snacks. A note says: *Had a last minute audition—so, so sorry had to leave you all alone. Will make it up to you. Miss you already.*

I take a twenty-minute shower in the claw foot tub and wipe little portholes in the steamed eyebrow window to watch three pigeons on the fire escape. One of them is almost silver, the same color as the outside, as the sky. She is the prettiest. I pretend I am a little girl. I make up a song. With the ballerina's black clay soap I scrub my winter skin. I scoop two fingers of her French shea butter conditioning treatment and coat my hair. I pat my face with her Dead Sea mask until it has caked and dried, until my mouth can't move.

–

My landlady lives below me with her daughter's family. I hear them through the floor as if we live together, which I guess is true. Her grandsons scream and eat bacon in the mornings. I can smell the crisping fat in my bedroom.

She pleads with them: Per favore!

Whenever I catch a glimpse of the little boys in the depths of their crowded apartment, they are dressed in superhero pajamas.

Mrs. Grioli is a widow and she cooks all day with the television on in the background. Usually it's Spanish soap operas, which is odd because I'm sure all she knows is Italian. When I get home hungover and pale on Saturday afternoons, she shuffles to the foot of the stairs with fresh fried calamari and meatballs, and even though I don't eat meat I take them all, still hot and wrapped in an oil-soaked paper towel.

Eat, eat, she coaxes.

I try to tell her about the clogged shower drain but she doesn't understand and I am too tired to show her what I mean.

–

One night I watch that movie where Billy Bob Thornton returns home after spending his whole life locked up in a mental hospital for hacking his mom to death, then befriends a little boy and saves him by committing another murder. I cry so much because I'm not kind enough. To myself, to anyone. Holding tight to my menagerie, holding myself at arm's length. Where is my softness? What kind of girl am I?

I listen to this podcast and it says: see a stranger, imagine their suffering, wish them love. Then do it with someone you don't like. Then do it with yourself. That's the hardest part, harder than you might think, if you're really doing it right.

—

Sophie bites my shoulder, wipes her fingers across my mouth. Asks me, Are you really here?

I don't have an answer. Don't know what that means.

I love you, she tells me, I love you, beautiful girl.

I need you too, I tell her.

I want to be bad. I want to be kind. I want to be beautiful. So I press her against me—my winter bandage, my new best friend. A girl with silver rings and a silver cigarette case filled with anxiety pills. Even her can I keep, up on the shelf with the rest of them?

But a few months pass and I can't ride the subway anymore without hurrying to the surface every four stops for air. Can't walk the High Line without feeling like I've lost the earth, like I'll fall into the sky and never stop spinning. Like my brakes are busted. I never get enough breath inside me. I cry on the stone steps of churches or on benches outside juice bars, hurrying back to my room before an attack sets in. I am someone who cries on the train. I am someone others try to ignore.

When I sleep I dream I'm upside down in a swimming pool, that I can't kick my legs down from where they are poking through the surface of the water. I dream of silent, shadowy hallways in the old house on the river where I grew up, or that I'm losing my teeth—they drop onto my tongue, crunch off between my fingers like hunks of hollow bedrock. All day I feel them in my mouth. My head buzzes, my left eye twitches. I tell Sophie she can't stay over anymore and soon I'm on my own again.

—

The abject is ambivalent—while it shatters it may also take us to the heart of our existence, define our identity, make us feel more alive. How alluring, this promise of heightened awareness. Longer looking, harder feeling. More more more.

—

On my walk to the gym I choke down half a bag of dried apricots for dinner. It's been a week since the big storm and lumpy heaps of leftover blizzard still clog up the streets. Car tires spin in deep tracks and wind spits crusted snow back up into the sky, into my boots, my eyes. Stiff, sparkling snowflakes dangle above the hookah shops and halal trucks, the discount dollar stores that smell like hot plastic; above hand-painted tavernas and yeasty bakeries, dusty lingerie stores displaying ancient girdles, Lebanese night clubs with blacked-out windows; above the steamy laundromats and fruit stalls spilling out onto the sidewalks, treacherous with oily puddles and rippled black ice. It's nearly February but Christmas music still plays, tinny and electric, almost unrecognizable, piped in through a speaker system that spans Steinway Street.

When I take off my gloves in the elevator my palms are already itching. Half a mile on the treadmill and my lips burn with histamine. I rake them with my teeth, my teeth like soft pillows. Now the heart is bumping around in the ears and when I look down the hands have swollen up like Minnie Mouse gloves. Stop the machine. Jog to the room with the stuff, the lockers. The face in the mirror is a skinned peach. Pull off shoes and socks because the soles of the feet are stinging. A woman is undressing in slow motion in front of me. Barefoot, I push open a stall door and vomit. My guts are whining, tight and high-pitched. All ninety-nine pounds too heavy to lift, so I slide down and let the cool tiles work their magic on my limbs, shoulder, right cheek.

Help, I say aloud and now I know that this is what it is like to really need help.

Then it is time to surrender, to recall childhood anthems: stop drop and roll, don't talk to strangers, don't play with matches, this is what you do when you are choking, this is why you wear a helmet, this is what you do when someone is having an emergency. Do the thing they teach you to do when things are the worst they could be.

A woman answers and everything sounds calm because the words won't come quick enough.

I ate something bad, I manage, it was the apricots, maybe. I ate a lot of them. I was so hungry.

It doesn't sound right. It sounds so stupid. And now I can't remember where I am.

Hold on, says the woman on the phone.

This is what it's like when your body wants to hold the poison back and away from your heart. Breath thick as steam. I close my eyes and wait for the ambulance. And I'm almost smiling. Someone is coming to save me. This is not so bad, I think. I'm in love with my petite organs, my little heart, the silky blood, how it all warns, how it wants to be encouraged. I have both shrunk and expanded; both lost self and become other, something bigger.

Three men are above me with deep voices and bulky gear. They lay hands on my red belly, my hot forehead, my calves.

Oh yeah, they say. They know what to do. They put a needle in my arm, a mask over my face. My pillow teeth start to chatter and suddenly I laugh.

The fluids are just cold, the men say.

Then the three of them pick me up and wheel me out into the night, lifting the chair over brown snow.

I'm thinking: I almost died. And still I can't stop smiling, because there is something sweet and loving, something that makes so much sense. I want to touch the objects in the ambulance. What are these for? What about this? Like a child. Like it's a rocket ship.

They tell me to relax; they check my pulse. It's just a van made by men, and the men just have equipment and other things that are really only plastic and metal. And it is regular voices talking about what could be any regular thing and regular men holding me, keeping me here, in winter, in Queens, on Earth.

In the narrow ER hallway I lie on the gurney for an hour until my breath comes back and my skin cools down. The space feels brown and yellow. Peeling and dated—hot with controlled panic. The woman from the clinic is there, of course. Like now this is her thing. Her hair comes swinging around the corner and at first I can't tell if she recognizes me. But why else would she be there? Her eyes are closed as she walks past my stretcher towards the front desk. I want to show her what I have discovered, what these men did for me, what my body did for me. It's all so real.

Can the fruit flies hear you yet? she whispers, like her mouth is right up to my ear, like the strings of her voice are knotting inside me, whipping up through her own shimmering throat to touch mine.

What? I say.

If you would just slow down, she tells me.

An ageless man comes in through the automatic doors wearing work boots, jeans dusted in white powder, and a Yankees sweatshirt. He can't speak English except to say that he is sick and that he took penicillin and it's not working.

Sounds like you have the flu, a nurse says with her arms crossed, looking down her nose from behind purple framed glasses. You can't just take penicillin once you have the flu. Where did you even get penicillin?

Down the hall behind a curtain someone is moaning.

It's my stomach it's inside my stomach, over and over.

I look at my phone and there is a text message from a strange number. It's one of the ambulance men: Just wanted 2 make sure ur doin ok and if u need anything just let me know. hope this isn't weird.

Of course it's weird. How could that not be weird? But what I'm thinking about is how he noticed me. He must have liked how little space I took up; starving, demure in lack. A vulnerability I have been so careful to hide.

—

All food goes next. Maybe it was sulfites. That's what the ER nurse said.

That, and you were very, very dehydrated. You're very underweight.

She handed me a sealed Epi-Pen and told me goodnight. I could see her feeling something—pity or distaste.

Now everything makes my lips itch. Everything I put in me, on me, is poison. I swallow six Benadryl a day. Maybe that's where the headaches are coming from. Carrying the Epi-Pen in my bag like a concealed weapon or a sex toy. A dirty secret that might go off, vibrate or explode. I have to talk myself out of panic all day.

On the commuter train to visit my father upstate I try to hold it together. Talking about my panic attacks, about my tonsils, is worse than not. Be the liar you can be. I eat a granola bar, same kind I've eaten for years, but something gets weird—my neck itches and I scratch and feel those bumps on my face. Stumbling towards the light of the train car's restroom, latching the door shut with shaking hands, pulling at my face in front of the mirror, moving the skin around for signs of reaction; examining, scrutinizing. What new betrayals are here? What new dangers?

See? See? I talk to my face. Nothing. There's nothing.

I rinse my hands in the little steel sink, throw cold water on my face and collapse on the floor with my head on my knees. I push a little white Klonopin out of its foil and let it dissolve on my tongue. I don't care about anything except not dying, not coming undone. Hardened clumps of soggy toilet paper, the sharp smell of blue toilet water: whatever this is has made me forget to be disgusted.

–

What is it that's so seductive about not taking up space? What have I been taught? The woman with extra weight has lost control. She's failed. The body betrays her mistakes, her weakness. But what's hard is that even though I know I've made a mistake—that somehow I did this, let myself get sick, and now something is terribly wrong—it appears as if I have done something right.

I've lost control of the inside. I've lost the fantasy that I ever had control. But on the outside I am something worth holding, worth looking at. I have the most perfect body he's ever seen.

—

The good thing is no one sees me up close. No one watches me shake when my skin tingles or when my mouth goes dry, or when I double check my wrists for hives while I'm eating. It's exhausting, being this afraid. But it's only my exhaustion, no one else's. I go to work, come home, sweat, prepare lunch for the next day. When it gets dark I drink wine in the shower, shoot up my nostrils with solution and watch yellow mucus drip down the drain. Then I go back to Manhattan and stay until some body takes me home or until I can't keep my eyes open.

Clothes don't fit me. I've lost the fold in my stomach, the roundness in my upper thighs. The nighttime boys ask me, Are you shrinking? They love it. They smile and hold my waist, give me bogies and beer and cab money. It's what I've always wanted. Smoke gets trapped beneath my monstrous tonsils for days—I can taste it when I yawn, my throat stretching as though it might crack like an old rubber band.

But whenever I close my eyes something is waiting, an ugly sob. The face of that woman with her giant eyes. And something white. Everything that is peaceful makes me cry, everything that is sweet, that is true. And maybe what's true is I don't want to get better.

Like Woolf knew: *There is, let us confess it—and illness is the great confessional—a childish outspokenness in illness; things are said, truths blurted out, which the cautious respectability of health conceals.*

—

If wallowing is like sex for depressives, bad sex is something like melancholia for me—pathological grieving over a loss not so easily identified. Or at least, not so easily said. I know this much: the salve of bad intimacy, like a confession, allows for the simultaneity of both presence and isolation.

Psychologists talk about emotional valence, to gauge the intrinsic attraction or aversion one is likely to have to others or to situations. What people would or wouldn't want to feel. And most people don't want to feel sad. Most people don't want to be around other people who make them feel bad. Happiness positive, sadness negative.

But you must know by now what I'm trying to say. What I mean about the overlap, the pleasure. How it becomes a part of your story, and how good it feels to have a story. Like how sometimes you might close your eyes to remember the melancholy cheer of twilight in August; copper leaves already crackling across the valley; a chill around your ankles at dusk, the endings of things. That specific kind of good and sad. Bass in your heart, smoke in your lungs, a little extra dope in your blood, someone's eyes on your body, other women waiting in other bars for a text message from those eyes. A blue, streetlight lit darkness, more lovable than you could ever be. Leaving in the morning because your story is about endings and desire. A privileged kind of loneliness.

Quiet, I will whisper in your ear one day, *I am remembering being lonely.*

—

Maybe it's obvious, the link between rupture and injury—an organ goes berserk, a spinal disc splits and leaks, or an Achilles tendon splays. Illness, on the other hand, might come upon us more like clouds than lightning. Like fog rolling in. And yet, doesn't it offer its own kind of rupturing? A fever pokes holes, deflates, makes things go pop. Things like roles and routines. Soon there are no names to call upon other than *ill*. I am sick, we tell others. And if months go by with still no answers, if no path appears to take you out of your body—to uncurl your thoughts from your chest, your guts—you might start to bang on the walls. You might start to push against your own malfunction, test the boundaries of your ruptured self; to reach over the glass for other peoples' secrets, for safety, for leverage; to air out your abject body like a secret itself. The shattering of the distinction between the self and the other.

I want everyone to see it, what's inside. I want their needles. I want their tongues. I want their sickness so I can call it ours.

—

The soap star's apartment smells like his dog. Damp and humid: a moldy pool house. Some Febreze. A carpeted hallway leads to his bedroom. He flicks on the overhead light and it appears as though there has just been an earthquake. I know. The first time my brother and I slept away from home without our parents was the night Los Angeles shook with the highest ground acceleration recorded in urban North America. I woke that morning to the walls cracking, the fridge puking its guts out, framed pictures dancing off their hooks.

Oh, he says. Some of my shelves fell down. I haven't put them back up.

He looks at me like, I'm sorry...? He's not sure how he should feel.

With our bodies we're both like, I'm sorry...?

There is a mountain range of clothing and paperback books—peaks and plateaus, no visible floor space, nowhere to walk. The comforter balled up on his bed is covered in dog hair. I can't leave because it's very late and he drove me out here in his car, some far eastern part of Brooklyn miles from a train.

Maybe I can help you, I offer, mostly because I want something to do.

No, no, no, he says, it doesn't matter.

He coughs into his elbow. He goes out to walk the dog and smoke a cigarette, and alone in the bathroom there is blood on my underwear, which is only very bad because now what am I going to do with him? I peer into the earthquake closet. A pair of women's boots is shoved back in the corner. It must have been her sunglasses in the bathroom, too. Her three black bobby pins in the soap dish.

Let's give him a blowjob. It takes less than two minutes.

Let's stare at his back tattoo in the darkness. His father's face inked into a crescent moon across his shoulder blade. Something about a man he feared and revered.

You want to know something crazy? I say softly. Sometimes when I fall asleep I get stuck, like I'm paralyzed but my mind is awake. And sometimes something else is there. Music, a guitar. Once, when I'd been crying, a woman sat on my bed. She touched my arm and I could see her hands were wrapped in rags, her fingernails were dirty, like she was from another time. But other people have it worse, you know. Like hallucinations that sit on them until they can't breathe.

What the fuck? he says. That is some fucked up shit to tell someone before they go to sleep. Jesus.

Then we are both silent. I listen to his dog circling and circling. How is it that she moves so steadily among the clutter? Light from a streetlamp swims in through the blinds. The woman, I think. It must be her.

In the morning he thanks me for the nightmares. I call myself a cab, take a cigarette from the bedside table, and wait outside on his stoop in the cold.

A few weeks later he sends me a message: What happened? Where have you been?

I give him the only answer I have.

I'm sick, I confess. It's this whole mystery.

–

The last doctor I see is the third throat specialist. One wall in his office is papered with glossy headshots of Broadway singers. He has a plastic, uncanny face. It isn't altogether bad. He wears a suit and tie while he dabs at the tender glands in my neck and chest. I talk for a long time, about the tests and the fevers, the rounds of steroids. I tell him almost everything.

He smiles. There are lots of weird viruses out there, he says. He tells me not to take any more medicine. To just get some rest. Be kind to yourself, he says. Slow down.

From the waiting room I call my father to ask for the five-hundred-dollar consultation fee.

That's all I can remember clearly. The doctor's shiny face, smiling and nodding as I spoke, the light touch of chilly fingers barely grazing my body.

But not too long after that the fevers stop and my tonsils recede like soft creatures back into the sea floor. I wake up in the mornings with energy, an appetite. I sleep through the night without soaking my sheets in sweat. A relief, of course.

But still. What was it I used to tell myself about how to be?

Something is always there: tremors of heat, fragility—like crystallized sugar, some thin membrane. I picture hardened shelves of crusty sand on beaches, the way they crumble. A headache sends a flutter of panic, fucks up my heartbeat, and when I let myself get lonely enough I'm still that person who knows what to do with my eyes, my mouth. I'm still that person who wants to shrink down so small that anyone could pick me up and carry me. I'm still that person, clumsy and violent, who wants to be covered up, anonymous, by some other body, to fall back among the sick, back into the lake tucked behind my apartment with plumes of my own blood and god knows what else.

—

Sons & Other Strangers

The Amtrak stops here almost every day, coming or going to California or Florida. Men and women on and off with roller luggage, with overstuffed backpacks, with duffel bags. Others stumble down the stairs and out into the hot wind for a smoke or a piss with just a few crumpled bills in their fists, squinting. Sometimes everyone is drunk, whole families, aunts and uncles with six young kids asking for french fries and burgers. Which we don't have. Most are alone though, these men who look like traveling preachers with pressed shirts and straw hats and awful ties, or wandering men who wear bandanas and work boots and who might have a glass eye, who seem to think they're good friends with everyone they've talked to since Dallas. They smell like travel, like reheated pastries.

My man, my man, they point to each other, get me a six-pack, my money's on the train.

They want cigarettes and shots of Jim Beam, and I have to tell them that we aren't that kind of bar and we don't have cigarettes and that there are no convenience stores anywhere close by, but that we have a nice white and a red to choose from and some local bottled beers in the fridge.

They want a cup of coffee for a dollar and we don't have that either. Nothing in the store costs less than $2.50. Not even the drip, and they roll their eyes or whistle and I don't blame them.

They need tampons and Tylenol and Pepto-Bismol; they ask for *junk food*, for puffed Cheetos and Skittles, for Butterfingers and Cool Ranch Doritos. They're in their pajamas, over-sized pink tee shirts that say *Princess*, or three-day-old clothes.

We have some kettle corn, I say, but they scrunch their noses.

We don't even sell lighters. But we do sell hand-painted desert-themed magnets and cold brew from Portland and tubs of Arizona honey and kombucha and pressed sandwiches with hand-pulled mozzarella and roasted chicken by the half or whole.

Let me get three of the cupcake, let me get two of the ham sandwich but I hate mustard and we only eat provolone. You got provolone at least?

A skinny woman with greasy brown hair and worn out platform clogs sits at the counter and wants to try all the beers on tap. She picks the Belgian ale and I pour it into a frosty glass and place it on a little black paper napkin in front of her. She takes a long drag from the foamy head, wipes her mouth with her hand and starts looking through one of her bags, looking and looking, pushing things to this side and that side. Her head moves in quick jerks, like a small bird.

A man sits beside her and orders a pepperoni pizza. He asks me how I'm doing. The woman talks to him as I clear tables and take sandwich orders and steam milk and cocoa and fill more pint glasses and weigh out pasta salad from the deli case. The man's food comes and soon the woman has a slice in her hand and she's nudged her stool up closer to him. He's nodding and chewing and pulling thick strings of melted cheese from between his lips. His fingertips are darkened with oil or dye or ink.

In the middle of the rush, a young man, maybe twenty, comes up to the register sobbing. He looks like my younger brother, tall with coarse blond hair and a bony face. But this kid is hunched over, holding his stomach, and the neck of his shirt is stretched out, wet and shiny, like he's been wiping his nose on it.

Please, he begs me, please I just want one more drink. They cut me off, he says.

He can barely stand.

My mother just died. She was all I had. They said I was too drunk. But what the fuck do they know. She just died. They just called me, and I never even got to see her.

I look up at him and I look around. But it's just me; everyone who works here is apparently gone. Snot is dripping down his face and I don't know what to do. So I say what comes out, which is I'm so sorry. And I tell him that I can't serve him either, there are laws, but that I am so, so sorry and that maybe he should just go home.

He says, Imagine if the only person who loved you died? Your mother. She's gone. This morning.

I can't imagine, I say, and it's true. But I really try try try to imagine. It's the least I can do. I think about what my mother would do.

Maybe you should go home, I say.

I don't have a home, he shakes his head. I'm staying with some people. I don't have anything.

I'm just really sorry, I say again. And then, Do you want something to eat?

Ok, he says, Ok, I guess I'll have a cookie. What kinds of cookies do you have? I want that chocolate chip cookie.

And he leans way over the counter with his whole body like he wants to lie down on it, tears still coming down his face. It feels like I want to touch him in his abandonment. I'm thinking about him eating that cookie, the way my brother would eat a cookie. I'm thinking about the vulnerability of pleasure, of eating; the terrible sadness of watching someone else's lonely comfort.

He pays for it, and I think, how could I be so cold.

I can't shake his face, not for the whole day. He makes a slow lap around the market before pushing himself through the door and out into the hovering twilight, maybe the longest twilight this boy has ever known.

I turn to check on the people at the far end of the bar just as the woman is following the man out the back with her three shopping bags on her wrists, beer still not paid for. I feel angrier than I probably should. I call out to her and ask if she forgot something. She tells me that she thought the man paid for her, but she knows I know she's lying and finally she just shrugs.

I don't have anything to pay for it with, she says.

I jog across the courtyard to the restaurant and get Billy, the manager, the ex-football star, and I leave it to him. He's annoyed with me somehow. Says I'm lucky he caught her.

After ten minutes the woman finds a credit card in her wallet and charges the beer and pretends to cry.

Once the train pulls away the market is quiet for nearly an hour. I dust wine bottles and drink coffee alone. I hold a mug in both hands until my warmth takes all its warmth away. I think about the boy with the dead mother. I think about how we do that, how our bodies pull the heat from other objects until those objects are cold. The adiabatic cooling of touch, of a substance decreased as it does work on its surroundings. And imagine, how hot the liquid must feel to the air.

I bite my lips until they are hard and ridged on the inside like wet dunes at low tide. And then there is my watch, and the wind, which I do and don't ignore.

—

Sorb
verb intr.:
    1. To take up and hold by absorption.
    2. To take up and hold by adsorption.

The difference between absorption and adsorption is this.

In absorption a substance is completely assimilated by another—sucked up, drawn in, taken in, blotted up, mopped up, sopped up. Both object and substance are changed. They have no choice.

But in the latter, one substance is deposited on the surface of another, accumulating and forming a thin film. This kind of binding is weak and reversible, scientifically speaking. No pores are filled. Nothing gets inside.

What I mean is how can I know what I have done? How can I know which processes I have been to whom—collecting, impermanent, on some already fleeting surface (the body, the mind), or sinking beneath it? It cannot be so simple as *knowing*. As *stranger*. Lover. Enemy. Friend. Who am I smeared on top of, a thin film, easily reversible? Who is inside me forever? Is one process kinder? Is there a difference? A better choice?

—

There's an upright piano in the coffee shop where I like to write, and today a girl wearing a wide-brimmed sunhat is suddenly standing over it. She pulls out the bench, sits down and sings. Where did she come from? It was silent just before. She riffs on the words: ...*mama is so, so very good lookin'*. The chords come after they should. She slaps the top of the piano with one cupped hand like it's a drum and pokes at the keys with other. Her voice is like a child's, undeveloped and strained, as though it were being pushed through feathers. But she is no child. She is tall and bony, her arms like undone coat hangers.

When she's finished, a man and a woman at one of the tables clap and the girl goes to them, laughing.

She says, Well yes, that's what I get into sometimes when I'm not doing my club music. Mm ch mm ch mm ch.

She drinks from a glass on the table, shaking the leftover ice while the three of them talk. Then she goes back up to the piano on its platform in the window and plays a few more chords. She likes to press the peddles—she's into the sostenuto—the way they sustain her sounds. She pauses, replays the chords she botched, patching up the melody where the wrong notes led her voice astray. She doesn't care, the living is easy. It's summertime. She's free.

It's early in the day, just after eleven. Her two friends have disappeared. Her accidental audience is me and a few men in matching plaid shirts. We go type type type on our laptops.

Outside: the locusts; their metallic hissing. The temperature has risen above 98, past 99, is hovering near 104.

Inside, a girl improvs on an old piano the same color as her hair.

While she plays, a man hangs his charcoal sketches on the walls of the coffee shop with tacks. His young son is holding a roll of duct tape, ripping off pieces and sticking them over his mouth. He marches around the tables and makes a sound like he's blowing into a kazoo.

–

At seven the brewer from Flagstaff with the beard comes to the cafe to change out his kegs. I tell him about the boy, how I've never seen anyone that drunk. I'm not sure if I'm being clear, if I'm saying the right thing. If I'm saying what I really mean.

Shit, he says. Rough day. He drinks two glasses of water and a pint of his own beer and then he's giving me his phone number.

My Russian scientist is the last customer before closing. He orders espresso with whipped cream. Today he wears a baseball cap and a dark suit.

Bella, he says with his heavy accent that makes me think of home. There are so few of those kinds of voices in the desert.

You look like a ballerina today, he says. If only I still had more hair. The ballerinas, ah! There are no women quite like them. With their long backs, just like you. When I live in the apartment on a hundred eighty six street, we used to take the ballerinas out dancing around Columbus Circle.

His eyes twinkle beneath thick black eyebrows, like he's someone who should be puffing on a cigar. He refolds his newspaper under his arm and stirs the espresso with a spoon before going outside to watch the trains.

The dancers were always the most beautiful. Up and down Lincoln Square. But this was when I was a boy, of course.

—

When I first moved out to the desert I kept thinking about a boy I knew briefly who was born here, in this town. He changed his name to Wyatt when he got to New York, so that's how he was listed in my phone. He was a model slash comedian. His jokes were so bad. Offensive, but also just not funny. I did my sleepy-eyed laughter when he read his tweets aloud to me in a dark restaurant—stuff about Mexicans and periods mostly. When he was in the bathroom I took two shots of whiskey at the bar. His face was probably the most symmetrical thing I'd ever touched. He talked a lot about the four-hour work week. He didn't eat bread or dairy. He lived in a railroad apartment above 186th street with two strangers while working nights in the Meatpacking, manning the doors at clubs with long lines. That's how I met him—cutting one of those lines.

The kitchen of the apartment where he lived was filled with ancient containers of spices that didn't belong to him. The whole place felt yellow and brown. Maybe that's what he liked about it; how it reminded him of home.

Once I lay in his bed for a full day waiting for him to touch me again. I'll never know what that day was like because there were no windows.

–

Just before the lunch rush a teenaged girl wearing three shades of black comes in and asks for an application. Her eyes are rimmed in black. She is very pale.

Does Xander still work here, she asks.

Who?

Xander? A little dishwasher, she says, and she holds her hand beneath her chin to show just how little he was. But no one named Xander works here, as far as I know, and I tell her.

Well anyway, she says, I really need a new job 'cause Walmart is killing me and I really wanna go back to college.

I stop folding napkins and hand her the form.

I'm working nights, she says. Do you know what that's like? In the morning I feel like my face is going to fall off. Have you ever wanted to rip your face off?

She laughs and laughs, slow and guttural, smearing her hand on the glass door on her way out.

–

Last night a friend told me about the wash. A place of firsts. Drugs
and blowjobs; pink lightning. The oily, creosote-laced heat before
a monsoon.

In the wash, she kept saying, in the wash, down in the dust.

I love this, I said, the wash!

I drank my wine and thought of where I used to go in the town
where I grew up. The town where I turned 13, 14, 15, 16, 17, 18 and
several other years even before those. No dust, no hot wind from
over the Catalinas. No lights from the cars on the overpass. Instead
I had the shadows of freshly paved cul-de-sac, the maze of an empty
corporate park.

Desert kids, I imagined, jerking each other off after sunset,
passing blunts and bottles of Southern Comfort beneath the eaves
of concrete bridges, their sneakers sinking into cooling mounds of
sand. Meet me by the mesquite tree where the parking lot ends at the
dried up riverbed. Like we're the first. Like it matters.

We were not as hidden as we thought, my friend said.

—

In *On Being Ill* Woolf wrote: *always to be understood would be intolerable.* And when I first read this I did not believe her. She must have meant the opposite. A facetious joke. After all, who can resist the gooey indulgence of feeling understood? As if it were a kind of loving.

But lately I wonder if Woolf wasn't more interested in calling out her separateness. Maybe she wanted us to understand that she in fact could not be understood. Reading and writing the other, perhaps, in order to read the self. There is pleasure in tracing the unknowable boundaries. A positive valence effect. Maybe we only look at the other to gauge the mileage, the outlines, the distance, finally unattainable in our separateness. And maybe there is power in that mystery.

I know this: always to be understood would be unbearable. Claustrophobic. Sometimes the performance is all that keeps me going. Once when I was young I flew to Miami on someone else's miles, someone guy's black American Express card. He asked me several times and finally I decided to see what would happen. I mean I knew what would happen. I knew what I would probably have to do. You can't use the ones who think they know you the way you can use those who never will.

—

On a Monday night the brewer from Flagstaff calls and I tell him to meet me at the beer garden.

I can't go there, he says. I just broke up with my girlfriend and they all know us.

How about the Dublin? I ask.

He says that sounds good, since he's never been. So we meet there, get a couple cans of Tecate, and sit outside on an empty, leafy patio. It's dark and so hot that I'm sticking to my jean shorts, yanking on the crotch to keep them from bunching up.

He tells me the facts: I'm actually a potter.

I know, I say. I looked you up.

I've been trying to leave that woman for a long time, he says.

He won't stop touching his beard.

It's late but we keep talking until I feel fuzzy in the face, and then we walk the quiet streets to the dive bar with the juke box where we play darts.

I'm going away, he says.

He's serious and soft-spoken but he does this dance when he gets a bullseye, which makes him confusing and silly and too vulnerable—vulnerable enough that I'm suddenly exhausted, can't keep my eyes open.

I have to move all her stuff back to Flagstaff, he tells me by my front door. Can I see you when I get back?

Maybe it's the white dust under his nails but I keep thinking about him even though there's nothing I really want.

Three days later he comes by my apartment with three bottles of wine from his ex-girlfriend's label and a ceramic mug of his own creation. It's nice, glazed in green and blue. But it's too much.

I want you to have this, he says. So I drop some pens in it show him I'm grateful.

We drink two of the bottles before he touches me, comes up behind me and puts his big arms around my waist. Ah. We kiss. It's pretty bad. So I get on top of him, but that's worse.

He keeps apologizing.

I really want this, I really want this, he keeps saying. It's just all this stuff. Everything just happened.

I don't care, I say. Whatever you want.

Which is true. I'm not even sure how he got in here, how I had this much wine.

Things used to be so easy. My body was once on its own, running the show. Making decisions and showing people a good time. Things are different. Lately my body just stands around and watches while I think. *I used to have such a good imagination. I used to be so tough.*

We lie on the rug and talk about his girlfriend some more. How she pushed him around. How he lost himself. I really listen. I make the room safe with my listening.

I'm going home to Ojai for a while, he tells me, like he's reassuring himself, repacking his things in his mind, stacking his newspaper-wrapped ceramics into boxes.

We stand on my bed in our bare feet and cover the wall with glow-in-the-dark star stickers until the real sun starts to come up from behind the Catalinas. We make a tiny galaxy, switch off the light and watch it grow.

Put them wherever you want, I tell him.

This is me being kind. He can sleep here. He can put his face right up to mine if he needs to, even if my face doesn't matter, even if I'm just spit and sounds. Even if he wishes he were with someone who really knows him, who he once told the whole truth to. Or most of it. I get it. I do.

But it's your wall, he says, like he really is concerned. How do you want it to go?

—

Today I wait for a long time, almost three hours, but no one touches the piano.

Instead, two men are planning an excursion.

One of them says, Elevation will be about a six or seven—six or seven thousand footer. Five days there, hike up to Machu Picchu. Photos, spiritual stuff. You know, what everybody wants.

—

I was not always like this, I tell a friend. I was not always so separate, so much inside myself, so outside the reach of others.

We are driving north in October, through the windy desert towards the mountains, where there will be soggy, burnt leaves to walk through and mist in the mornings. We scream along to The River and naturally this makes us want to smoke cigarettes, feeling nostalgic for a story that is and isn't ours. I slip two Parliaments out from a pack stashed in the console, and we blow smoke through the open window slits. Little gusts of evening air catch in my throat.

He says, Look, I know what it's like. Here's an example: for a long time I thought I had my person. And now. It's just like this trajectory.

He moves his hands out and up from his body like he's carving a fork in the road, like he's parting a wave.

But where does it end, this moving away from everyone else? The scariest part, he says, is that it's a choice. You can either keep moving away or not. At some point you're probably going to have to decide.

When I try to picture what not moving away looks like, it doesn't seem like a choice at all, not a choice I could actually make. I watch his hand, how he's drooped his wrist over the steering wheel, the smoldering Parliament balanced between his fingers. The way you are supposed to do it. The kind of thing that could really make you want to know somebody's secrets, to slide beneath the stock gesture and get inside, to see what you can make their eyes do when they surrender against your mouth.

—

In an interview Marina Abromović says she is three different kinds of person: a strong-willed daughter of political revolutionaries, a needy and frightened child, and someone else—someone spiritual and present, floating above her human weaknesses.

She says she likes that last person the best. But that it's ok to be all three.

It's ok, she says. I forgive myself.

—

I wake up in the pararescue's bed, palm fronds shuffling and chattering against the outside wall. This is Tucson in mid-November. The pararescue is awake too, staring up at the ceiling. He yawns, covering his mouth with his elbow and asks how comfortable I am with needles, how I feel about putting in an IV. He wants someone to cure his hangover. He needs someone to shoot him up with saline solution.

Not comfortable at all, I tell him. I have to laugh, I am so turned on.

But we are not touching. I'm wearing my clothes from last night, from work, where he picked me up with some military buddies after my bar shift and took me line dancing across Fourth Avenue at the dive with the tire swing and the canopy of bras. He knew all the steps—how to lift and hitch and shuffle. Had perfect rhythm in his hips, his feet. When he flipped me upside down my underwear was exposed to the crowded room. I was aware (through the whiskey I had already drunk) that this was funny and that I liked it. I rested on the tire swing, holding a beer close to my chest with one hand, and watched him move other girls around the floor, their lips parted and smiling. When he was tired we shared an American Spirit on the porch. I flicked and flicked with my thumb, though there was no ash. The desert air was cold, my cheeks hot. We were both sweaty at the hairline. His forehead glistened in the light of a neon Corona sign—deep pores, grayish dry patches around his young eyes when he grinned, the sprays of handsome crow's feet. He was only twenty-two. His damage endeared him to me. By now it is no surprise: I am easily flattered and easily endeared, which I both dislike and cherish in myself. Pride is just on the other side of shame.

Later we fell asleep talking. The darkness was grainy, the fuzzy channel on a television screen, the kind from my childhood. I remember him saying that he was not afraid to die. That his life had been good and he felt blessed to have pushed his body so hard, to have seen the world. He had jumped out of hundreds of planes, had saved many lives. He might have taken some—he said he wasn't certain. He could survive anywhere in a tent, in the snow. He believed in heaven but not hell. He loved his mother, who had raised him on her own, and planned to buy her a house in Santa Fe. I stayed mostly quiet, listening.

Now in the weak morning light I can see his upended snowboard and an open medical duffle bag packed with latex gloves and gauze and tubing. There must be syringes inside, too. The kid is prepared for disaster.

When he gets up to take a shower I walk one dusty block home with my head bowed into a gust of wind, passing a stray kitten before it slips into the narrow space between two buildings. We are neighbors, me and the pararescue. I'd be able to see his front door from my high-rise window, if my window faced west rather than east.

Yesterday he brought me to the wind tunnel, a surprise, driving north to the flatlands of Eloy in a brand new military-issued Subaru hatchback, beaming with his secret until we reached the airfield.

Look up, he said.

We sat in the grass and watched rainbow parachutes float in, appearing in the bright blue sky as dots, then smudges, then haloed appendages gliding towards the ground. The hum of airplane motors; the thin, tinny shouts from above; and closer, the whoosh and flap of nylon, the thud and heavy patter of feet struggling against momentum to find land. It was warm enough that I took off my sweatshirt and tied it around my waist.

Beyond the field at the edge of a large gravel parking lot was the wind tunnel, a forty-foot inverted cone built to stimulate the sensation of falling through the sky.

This is where you'll learn to fly, he said.

We signed waivers. A boy in a red jumpsuit gave us our own jumpsuits, helmets, goggles. In a windowless classroom I lay face down on padded table. The boy in the red jumpsuit told me to arch my back; he bent my knees into place with his hands, positioned my

ankles. He taught me three different hand signals, which I imme-
diately forgot.

You're a natural, said the pararescue. He waited patiently in one
of the plastic chairs.

When you get in there you have to relax, the other boy told me.
Jump up and onto the air and relax, breathe. Watch my face—I will
show you what to do.

But it is impossible to imagine falling through the sky without
ever having done it. You cannot be prepared for the force, the end-
less wind rippling over the skin of your hands, loosening your lips
into a manic, ballooning smile. Air was out there somewhere—I
could feel it all around. But it would not come inside. Instead it
made a seal over my mouth and nose. Spit and snot flew back against
the helmet, the goggles. I grabbed for the column wall like a pan-
icked child at the edge of a swimming pool, pulling myself out to
stand on the grate beyond the arched entrance.

I can't breathe in there, I tried to say over the roar of the fan,
my eyes bulging and shifty.

What do you mean, yelled the guide, who was somehow now
standing vertically on the net above the wind stream. He was genu-
inely confused.

Just breathe. Relax.

He moved his hands close to his chest and away again as if to
remind me that this is what air could do on its own.

Generations of families, children and grandmothers in thick
white orthopedic shoes, were watching from the set of bleachers
beyond the plexiglass. The paramedic was watching, waiting, giving me two thumbs up. The guide in the red jumpsuit was waiting,
bored. This is what these boys liked, what they did with their bodies. I had no choice. I tried again, taking a breath before throwing
myself back inside, the guide tugging on my sleeve, settling me into a
semi-balanced levitation on my stomach. I lifted my face and sipped
the air, quick and shallow. I was moving up and down. Gliding side

to side. And I almost stopped wondering about my snot and where it was. Or if there was drool on the jumpsuit.

Then the guide gave me a high five and signaled for me to exit, and the medic took his turn, floating beautifully, like a ghost might do, sitting upright as if in an invisible chair. The boys fell into a kind of choreography they seemed to already know, some kind of dance they'd memorized.

You want to go together? the guide yelled. Want to come in with him? he asked, joining his hands together, signaling for some sort of union.

But I shook my head.

When it was all over the boy pulled himself sideways out of the column and put his helmet close to my helmet and said something about being proud. He squeezed my hand and I thought about being fearless. How I wanted to be fearless like him. How I had never known anyone so fearless.

Back in town I brushed the knots out of my hair and changed into a pair of jeans. The boy propped me up on the back of his motor-cycle and gave me his motorcycle helmet. Holding onto him—his ribs pressing against my small breasts when he inhaled, the motor's guttural cough between my legs, the delicious shifting pockets of warm and cool breeze as we sped towards the mountains—I felt all the things I'd imagined one would feel on the back of a boy's motor-cycle in the desert. We ate lunch at the upscale open-air mall beside an outdoor fire pit filled with glass beads and blue flames. I ordered white wine. The boy ate a slab of chicken parmesan with a fork and knife. Then he dropped me off at work and later we went dancing.

Nothing else happened—that's how I'd describe it. Nothing else happened, though I'd followed him home, which was also on the way to my home. I don't remember much after that except the talking and the sensation of that there was a cobweb between us, fragile strands of inexperience or disinterest or something else. That it was my duty to persevere and to keep it from tearing.

I woke up hungover, wearing most of my clothes.

It's jarring after such saturation not to hear from someone like that again. I follow a longer bicycle route to and from campus to avoid passing his front door. I think about what it would take to require painkillers, what kind of weird sleep I'd have to endure to text him and ask because I know he has everything. Then maybe he'll want to take me places again, I think. Maybe he'll remember what I look like, or whatever it was that had drawn him to me in the first place. But the situation feels heavily irreconcilable, desperate. A transference already taken place. A misplaced emotion on an unwilling subject. The worst kind of defeat. These are the facts—I push them around in my head:

1. The kid was into God and guns.
2. I thought him at once naive and articulate.
3. His arguments about guns were convincing. Maybe because he also listened to folk rock.
4. This made me insecure.
5. He probably knew I could never really love him because of the gun thing and the God thing.
6. This probably also made him know he could never love me.
7. That, and he was much, much younger.
8. That, and we were both leaving Tucson soon.
9. He was very focused. He had specific goals, a five-year plan.
10. This made me think I wasn't focused at all. That I was lost.
11. Which made me feel old and also young.
12. He probably hated that.
13. I wasn't one hundred percent sure that I even liked him.
14. I had humiliated him.
15. He had found some of my published work online—stuff about irreverent blow jobs and other boys.
16. This was a new phenomenon. My writing had only recently become public. No potential friend or lover had ever read my stories without knowing me first.

17. It made him nervous—he had said that, in so many words. My body made him nervous. He had said that, too.

18. Just please don't write a story about me, he had said. I don't want to become a story.

19. Had I gained weight since we met?

20. A gay friend thought he was definitely a little gay.

21. He paid for everything: sushi, lunch, drinks, coffee, muffins, wind tunnels.

22. He thought I was sexy—he told me that.

23. He shook when we kissed.

24. He wanted to teach me how to fly.

25. He wanted me to ride on his motorcycle. Or maybe he was just riding his motorcycle with me on it.

26. He didn't like to wear the helmet on his motorcycle because it wasn't risky enough.

27. But he wanted me to wear one. Or maybe there was just nowhere else to put the helmet.

Then a week before Christmas, a Wednesday, I am at a pub in the barrio reading a story about a one-night-stand with an actor who asked if he could keep his potted ferns at my apartment while he went to Baltimore to be an understudy in a production of Othello.

An artist projects slides on the wall, photographs of deserted gas stations dripping with silver tinsel.

The tinsel makes shadows on my face like rain on a car window at night, and on the faces of tipsy graduate students packed into the bar.

Another writer reads a reimagining of a fairytale about a half-fish woman, doomed to be a mermaid forever if her lover catches her bathing with her fins exposed.

We try to address the existential loneliness in the impossibility of knowing anyone. (This is the description on the event flier.) The unbearable discomfort of being known and not, the weirdness and sexiness of hasty intimacy; plants, fins. Secretly I consider the wind tunnel, too. How I had wanted to own our differences, for the boy to hold them out to me so I could claim them up close. How I have never stopped trying to fill the lack that comes from being a lone self.

When I see the pararescue out of the corner of my eye I stumble, say hat lamp instead of heat lamp, which was what I had written. I scan my body—I'm wearing a tight skirt. My ass looks tight; my waist looks small.

Afterwards people clap. The kid walks through the crowd and clasps his hands behind my back. I am nearly his height.

You remembered, I breathe, leaning back, away from his face. I was wondering what happened to you.

The heat of the wine rises up my chest, my face.

I still want to learn to shoot a gun, I hear myself say.

And the next day he takes me. The shooting range is thirty minutes southeast of downtown. No signs—the kid drives from memory, turning off Route 10 and driving slowly along a dirt road through low desert brush.

One two. Three. Four five. Carefully placed gunshots.

Several picnic tables are lined up beneath a long corrugated tin roof. Three men and one woman are hunched over rifles, holding up handguns with their arms outstretched, aiming out across a sand pit.

A beat up trailer is perched on cinder blocks; a hand-drawn sign marks it as OFFICE. The boy parks and goes inside, emerging a minute later to ask if I have any cash. Cash only.

Of course, I say. Is this enough?

I take thirteen dollars from my wallet, which is all I have.

He goes in a second time and comes out with two paper targets shaped like human silhouettes—broad shoulders and buzz cuts. The boy shakes his head, laughs, describes the obesity of the man inside, the mountains of stuff—he can't even say what the stuff is, just lots of it.

The smell, he says, fuck.

Then the boy opens the trunk of his Subaru and his face becomes tight and serious. Much more serious than the day at the wind tunnel. He rolls up the sleeves of his windbreaker and I can see his blue tattoos.

Shooting a gun is a state of mind, he tells me. It's a violent act. You have to get tough, be aggressive.

The trunk is full of ammo and emergency medical equipment. He pulls out a long black case with a military assault rifle nestled inside and a smaller black case that holds a black hand gun.

I am tough, I say, smiling.

But I have never seen a gun in real life.

We put on noise-cancelling headphones and he picks a shooting lane on the far end away from the others, setting up our targets when a ceasefire is called.

He tells me the rules: Do NOT cross this line. Do NOT take off your headphones.

Then he lays down on his stomach, tucking the assault rifle beneath his body, and opens fire.

It seems to go on for a long time, his shooting. I turn slightly on my heels and watch two men at the other end of the range. They look like brothers from far away. The air is dusty with displaced sand. The landscape is bright, the wind cool, and apart from sporadic gunshots, it is very very quiet.

Then the boy is done. He stands and holds my fingers, positioning them around the mechanisms, demonstrating how to stand, touch the trigger with a light finger.

Breathe in, breathe out, lean into the butt, pull—you don't need to jam it.

I do what he says. The gun is heavy and he has me rest it on a waist-high cement block.

One. Two. Three, four, five, six.

A few puffs of sand explode beyond the wooden targets. My shoulder stings from the backfire.

Ow, I say, and he laughs.

Keep going. You're good! Really. I'm impressed.

I fold over the rifle once more, trying to make my body look the way he told me to make it look, or the way the boy's body had looked. It was just a posture, it was like anything else.

Gaze fixed on the center of the farthest target, I feel the para-rescue standing safely behind me. Feel him loving and hating the gun he had given me, loving and hating his own stocky body. And somewhere in between this I feel, finally, both his immediate care and complete ambivalence towards me. How easy he makes it look.

I am not nervous anymore. I am relieved. What I mean is that it's all over, and no one got hurt, not really. Not at all, actually. Truthfully, didn't he give me so much?

I let him watch me tap the trigger, my own lips tightening against my own teeth. He takes out his phone and aims it at my body. In a few days I will be far away, back in New York. Eventually I will forget and then remember that morning with the IV, when he almost needed me. I will write it down, will recall him intimately, insofar as our unknowability allows. I will send my friends the video he took of me shooting the rifle, and then later I will send it to other boys, so that they will also understand, so they will see how tough I am, how fearless. Someone once stood behind me and recorded the proof.

—

Acknowledgments

Many humble thanks to Chris Cokinos, Aurelie Sheehan, Nicole Walker, Kate Garrick, and my wise and patient friend Nick Greer, all of whom generously helped me through various stages of birthing this very tiny piece of myself into the world. Thank you to my parents—I love you more than I can ever say. And thank you to all the humans who might recognize themselves in these pages.

The phrase, "I used to have such a good imagination, I used to be so tough," comes from Tracey Emin's 1997 monoprint by the same name. All Jacques Derrida quotes come from his essay "Archive Fever: A Freudian Impression," published in *Diacritics* in 1995. The Pierre Auguste-Renoir quote on page 23 was found on a plaque beside his painting, "Tete," at the University of Arizona Museum of Art in spring 2014. All Virginia Woolf quotes and references come from her essay "On Being Ill." On page 27, the Anne Anlin Cheng references come from her 2011 book, *Second Skin: Josephine Baker & the Modern Surface*, published by Oxford University Press. On page 28 the John Berger reference comes from his 1979 BBC series "Ways of Seeing." Helaine Posner is quoted on page 30 from her 2005 book *Kiki Smith*, published by Monicelli Press. Roland Barthes is quoted on page 34 from his book *A Lover's Discourse*, translated by Richard Howard. All Julia Kristeva quotes and references can be found in Rina Arya's 2014 book, *Abjection and Representation: An Exploration of Abjection in the Visual Arts, Film and Literature*, published by Palgrave Macmillan. On page 56, the Wayne Koestenbaum quotes come from his book *The Queen's Throat: Opera, Homosexuality, and the Mystery of Desire*, published by Da Capo Press in 1993. The Marina Abramović references on page

93 are taken from the 2012 documentary *The Artist is Present*, directed by Matthew Akers. Definitions of the word *nepenthe* is a composite adapted from entries according to *Merriam-Webster* and *Dictionary.com*. The definition of the word *sorb* is adapted from *Merriam-Webster*. A version of "This One Long Winter" appears in *Fourth Genre Vol 19, No 1*. Other excerpts appeared in *Redivider, The Los Angeles Review, Hobart*, and *Hippocampus*.